The CORRUPTION OF THE CLERGY

Money, Tithing & Paid Pastors

The CORRUPTION OF THE CLERGY

Money, Tithing & Paid Pastors

DON BRITTON

Dedication

This book is dedicated to all the good and decent true Christians who have been misled by the modern teachings flooding the church today through all the false shepherds who are using their position for the unjust gain of money, power, and the approval of man, rather than for the approval of God. These are men who look after their own best interests rather than that of the people they are supposed to serve. May this book be an eye opener for anyone who reads it, and may you find the truth that sets you free.

Don Britton
Christianmyths.org@gmail.com
www.christianmyths.org

The Myth of the Tithe

From the multitude of sermons on "**_tithing_**" you would get the impression that God had filled the Bible with hundreds of verses on paying the tithe to the church. But the fact is that there are **_fewer than twenty verses_** in the whole Bible that talk about the tithe and almost all of them are in the Old Testament and all of them are associated with the **_Old Testament Jewish law_**. It seems, in some churches, that a tithing message comes up every few Sundays as if that is one of the main things God has on His mind. Many Christians have **_been beaten down_** with this message and left to feel guilty, if for some reason, they could not come up with the ten percent to put in the plate. It seems that many preachers stress that the tithe should be paid even before a past due mortgage or an unexpected medical expense. But **_what is the tithe_**? **_To whom was it to be paid_**? **_What was the purpose of the tithe_**? Does it have anything to do with the church today? Did any of the New Testament churches pay tithes? Did Paul instruct any of the churches to pay tithes? Let us find out if the modern teaching on tithing is a **_biblical truth or a myth_**?

"I had to pay my tithe!" That is what **_everybody in church_** used to tell me. I have heard it from every "Christian" financial counselor I have ever talked with, and from every church I have ever been a part of, in my thirty-nine plus years of walking with God. I have heard a multitude of messages on **_tithing_** from many preachers. It sometimes seemed that a sermon on tithing would come up every time the building mortgage payment came due. I have heard so much on tithing from ministers that I used to get the impression that God was ***more concerned*** with tithing than He was with just about anything else. In fact, I used to have the impression that the subject of tithing was all over the Bible and that it was one of the main topics of the New Testament—that is, until I ***studied*** it out for myself!

So, is the law of tithing a requirement for a Christian who is led by the Holy Spirit in his giving or is it just another ***tradition*** handed down to us from the ***teachings of men***? I can find ***no scripture*** to support tithing for the church. Read further and find out why.

> *And their reverence for Me consists of tradition learned by rote— **(thoughtless repetition)**. (Isa. 29:13)*

Remember that tradition learned by rote is religious tradition learned by doing the same things again and again as you go through the same motions ***over and over again, week after week, without giving any serious thought*** as to why you are doing it. Why don't church members ask why their pastor teaches ***law and grace*** at the same time? The tithe is of the ***law*** and grace is of ***Christ***. Why do men who have a doctorate degree in Bible theology teach this? But week after week, virtually most all of the churches in America are ***tithing over and over again*** because of the teachings of pastors and the traditions of men that have taken over and very few seem to notice.

Religious tradition does ***invalidate*** (render useless) the Word of God when it is practiced without correct biblical instruction as a basis for doing so. Does the Bible teach that the New Testament Church should preach and ***collect tithes*** or is it just another one of those ***myths*** most everyone believes without any regard for the Scriptures?

First of all, we need to find out ***what the tithe is*** and then ***why it was needed***.

*Thus, all the tithe of the **land**, of the **seed of the land** or of the **fruit of the tree**, is the Lord's; it is holy to the Lord.* (Lev. 27:30)

*"And to the sons of **Levi** (priests), behold, I have given all the tithe in Israel for an inheritance, in return for their service which they perform, the service of the **tent of meeting**.* (Num. 18:21)

*"For the tithe of the sons of Israel, which they offer as an offering to the Lord, I have given to the **Levites** for an inheritance; therefore, I have said concerning them, 'They shall have **no inheritance** (not allowed to own land) among the sons of Israel.'"* (Num. 18:24)

"You shall surely tithe all the produce from what you sow, which comes out of the field every year." (Deut. 14:22)

So here it is obvious that the tithe was given to the **_Levitical priests_** who served in the tent of meeting and later the temple. The Levites were **_not allowed to own land_** by which they could raise livestock and crops for food. Therefore, they were to eat from the tithe of the crops and livestock donated by everyone else. Take note of this fact—the tithe was **_never money_**. It was always **_produce_**, **_livestock_** or **_some kind of food_**. The main purpose of the tithe was to **_feed the Levites_** because they had no land to produce their own food and it was also used to help widows and orphans.

But there was another way the tithe was to be used:

*"And **you shall eat** (the tithe) in the presence of the Lord your God, at the place where He chooses to establish His*

*name, the **tithe of your grain**, your **new wine**, your **oil**,
and the **first-born of your herd** and your flock, in order
that you may learn to fear the Lord your God always. "And
if the distance is so great for you that you are not able to
bring the tithe, since the place where the Lord your God
chooses to set His name is too far away from you when the
Lord your God blesses you, then you shall **exchange it for
money**, and bind the money in your hand and go to the
place which the Lord your God chooses. "And you **may
spend the money for whatever your heart desires, for
oxen, or sheep, or wine, or strong drink, or whatever
your heart desires**; and there **you shall eat** (the tithe) **in
the presence of the Lord your God and rejoice, you and
your household.**" (Deut. 14:23–26)*

It is obvious that the tithe was **not money** since it had to be exchanged for money in order to make the trip. And since some preach the tithe as if it is for today, shouldn't they also tell you about this part—**that you don't always have to bring your tithe to them**, but sometimes you are supposed **to eat and enjoy your tithe with your family**?

More than likely, you have **never heard a sermon** teaching that you could take your own tithe and spend it on yourself and your family in order to **rejoice before the Lord** so that you would learn to **fear the Lord** your God. You see, the Lord is the one who gives you everything and He can take it away as well! Do you wonder why your pastor **never uses this verse on tithing**?

Did you know that there are 1,189 chapters in the Bible? Did you also know that out of those 1,189 chapters there are 31,173 verses containing about eight hundred thousand words? Consider this, out of the eight hundred thousand Hebrew and Greek words used, only **thirty-five times** do we find the words "tithe, tithes, or tithing" in the whole Bible and in fewer than **_twenty verses_**! That is not the impression most preachers leave about tithing and those thirty-five words are only found in **_sixteen locations_** in the Bible.

In addition to that, only four of those locations are found in the New Testament and none of these are instructing us to pay tithes. Did you also know that there is **_no record_** in the Bible of any church member **_ever paying tithes or being instructed to do so_**? So, who started that **_tradition_**? It certainly wasn't Jesus or any of the apostles. Did you know that there is **_no instruction_** written by any of the apostles to any of the churches to collect tithes or for any of the members to pay tithes?

Why would the tithing of crops and livestock be needed any longer since the Levitical priesthood was **_abolished_** with the death of Jesus? Why would tithing be needed any longer since everyone now is allowed to **_own land_** and provide his own food? And since Jesus abolished the priesthood and temple sacrifice, He also eliminated the need for the storehouse to keep the crops and livestock that would be eaten by the Levitical priests and given to the widows and orphans. So, is it any wonder that **_no one_** in the New Testament collected tithes, paid tithes or taught anyone to do either? So why do so many churches now teach that we have to pay tithes today? Could it be that the traditions and teachings of men have **_invalidated the Word of God_** just as the Scriptures said? Could it be that this teaching is **_self-serving to most preachers_** to fulfill their own goals, including securing their **_own income_** and funding the many programs they want or maybe to build a big and expensive building to bring **_glory to themselves_**?

Do you wonder why most all tithe teachers of today **_only_** use the verses below to teach about the tithe, while leaving out the other ones listed above?

> *"Will a man rob God? Yet you are robbing Me! But you say,*
> *'How have we robbed you?' In tithes and offerings. "You are*

cursed with a curse, for you are robbing Me, the whole
nation of you! "Bring the whole tithe into the storehouse, so
*that there may be **<u>food</u>** (**<u>something to eat</u>**) in My house*
(for the temple priest), and test Me now in this," says the
Lord of hosts, "if I will not open for you the windows of
heaven and pour out for you a blessing until it overflows."
(Mal. 3:8–10)

The storehouse was in the temple building, and the tithe was kept there to feed the Levites who served there. So what does that have to do with **<u>the church today</u>**? Aren't we the temple of God now? Why do ministers still preach **<u>law and grace</u>** at the same time? Isn't it really about the **<u>money</u>**? Money for programs, buildings, and **<u>especially for the preacher's salary and living expenses</u>**? And since the tithe never was about money to begin with and since the priesthood has been abolished and the storehouse is no longer used, why would any modern preacher teach a Christian believer that he had to tithe, that is, if the preacher used the **<u>Bible</u>** to teach from? Unless it is just about the desire for the **<u>money</u>**, because it certainly is **<u>not about the truth</u>**. Remember, the tithe was **<u>never about money</u>**, but was **<u>always about food</u>** for the temple priest and the needy.

But are we ever to give? Of course, we are, but not according to the **<u>letter of the law</u>**. Let each man be **<u>led by the Spirit</u>** and give as he has purposed in his own heart. And we should be careful **<u>to what</u>** and **<u>to whom</u>** we give. Our giving should be as it was done in the early church, which was mostly to **<u>help those in need</u>**. Today it could also be used to spread the Word of God. But it shouldn't be used for fancy buildings, useless religious programs and for **<u>paying preachers</u>**. See the next chapter so you will understand better what the Bible says about this.

> *Let each one do just as he **has purposed in his heart**; not*
> *grudgingly or under compulsion; for God loves a cheerful*
> *giver.* (2 Cor. 9:7)

You see, this is a **heart** thing not a law thing. The law causes people to **give under compulsion**. Giving under compulsion is giving under **pressure, out of force or out of fear of being cursed**. This is exactly what the tithe preachers have been doing all along, putting **pressure** on members to pay the tithe using the book of Malachi to **threaten members into giving or being cursed**. They have been using fear and guilt to **extort** money out of members for centuries. This is not the way of Jesus or any godly shepherd.

> *For all who are being **led by the Spirit of God**, these are*
> *sons of God.* (Rom. 8:14)

If you are being **led by the Spirit**, you are **not under the law**. So, giving is a heart thing directed by the Holy Spirit and tithing is of the law for the purposes we have already revealed. I cannot believe that the Spirit of God would have you to give your money to a church or preacher when you need to **feed your family first, pay your mortgage or you see someone in need and choose to help them**.

> *For as many as are of the **works of the Law are under a***
> ***curse**; for it is written, "**Cursed is everyone** who does not*
> *abide by all things written in the book of the law, to*
> *perform them." Now that **no one** is justified by the Law*
> *before God is evident; for, "The righteous man shall live by*
> *faith." However, the **Law is not of faith**; on the contrary,*
> *"He who practices them shall live by them.* (Gal. 3:10–12)

Since tithing is one of the ***works of the law***, you are actually in danger of ***being cursed*** if you try to please God by paying the tithe as a legal obligation (ten percent), being under ***compulsion***, or trying to keep the law, rather than giving ***as the Spirit leads you by faith***. The preachers who preach and collect tithes are committing an ***evil act*** by putting members under the ***threat of the law*** and by teaching a lie.

So, why would you tithe according to the law since it is not giving by faith but ***only legalism*** practiced by ***rote***? Also, why would you not give according to the leading of the ***Holy Spirit by faith***? Who did Jesus and the apostles teach us to give to anyway? Was it not the ***poor and the brothers and sisters in the body of Christ who were in need***? We were ***never taught to give to preachers*** anywhere in the Bible. We should only give to anyone the Holy Spirit leads us to, but not according to a law imposed upon us by preachers!

We should also give some money to the ***true church***. The true church does need finances for the ***cost*** of promoting the gospel as well as the cost of a simple meeting place and the few expenses that go with that, and also to help the poor. The true church ***does not need*** to have a paid staff, but only ***sincere volunteers***. There were ***no paid ministers or paid staff members*** in the New Testament church. Even the money collected then was used for ***helping those in need, like the widows, the poor, and the orphans, but not for paying preachers or building fancy buildings***.

Obviously, the modern teachings on tithing are nothing more than ***falsehood***. They are teachings of men that have been handed down to us for the ***purposes of men***. This tradition has ***robbed*** many widows and poor people by ***extorting money*** from them, money they often could not afford to pay, by preachers who ***falsely teach*** that they must obey the "Law", or they will be cursed. Sadly, many dear souls who struggle to make a mortgage payment and feed their children are under the same ***false impression*** that they must give ten percent of what they earn to the church, so the ***preachers can be paid*** and build fancy buildings for their own glory. This false teaching has resulted in **_many feeling guilty or fearful_** as well as coming under condemnation for feeding their children and paying for their home **_first_**, when they did not have enough left over to pay the ten percent to the church. This modern teaching on the tithe is **_outrageous and a great lie_**!

Jesus would never rob or pressure the poor or anybody for money nor did any of the Apostles make anyone feel guilty for not being able to pay a "tithe". None of the Apostles **_ever even mentioned the tithe_**.

> *"Woe to you, scribes and Pharisees, hypocrites, because **you devour widows' houses**, even while for a pretense you make long prayers; therefore, you shall receive **greater condemnation**."* (Matt. 23:14)

How many widow's houses and poor people's limited and needed incomes have **_been robbed_** by the tithe teachers? Have you ever wondered if the preaching of the tithe has anything to do with **_preachers being paid_**? That raises another question. Are preachers supposed to be paid? Is it biblical to pay preachers?

The answer is in the next chapter.

This is what Paul the apostle did for his income:

> *For you yourselves know how you ought to **follow our example**, because we did not act in an undisciplined manner among you, nor did we eat anyone's bread **without paying for it**, but with **labor and hardship** we kept **working night and day** (making tents) so **that we might not be a burden to any of you; not because we do not have the right to this** (to eat food), but in order to offer ourselves as a model for you, that you might **follow our example**. For even when we were with you, we used to give*

*you this order: if **anyone** (anyone includes preachers) will*
*not work, **neither let him eat.***
(2 Thess. 3:7–10)

The right Paul referred to was to **eat food**, **not collect money** from anyone for himself. And Paul certainly did not pass a collection plate and collect tithes from anyone! If the principle of "**will not work, neither let him eat**" was followed today there would be a lot of hungry preachers.

Here is another point about **pastors and tithes** . Often pastors **judge people** by whether they pay their tithes or not. I know of a case where a pastor **billed an absentee member** for his tithes like it was an accounts receivable in a business. I know of another case where a pastor **would not visit** a critically ill member of his church, at the hospital, because **she had not paid all of her tithes**. I know of another case where a pastor would not allow a godly poor church member to teach a bible study because he was behind on his tithes. I also know of a pastor who first checked the church records to see if a certain member was **current with his tithes** when that member began to have some type of crisis in his life. When that member was found to be late on his tithes, the pastor then **blamed him** for the trouble he was having, saying it was because he had not paid all of his tithes to the church. Jesus said **do not let** the left hand know what the right hand is doing concerning giving. **It is not the pastor's business what anyone is giving, but only God's**. Jesus instructed us to give in secret and to not to be noticed by others.

"Beware of practicing your righteousness before men to be
*noticed by them; otherwise you have **no reward** with your*
*Father who is in heaven. "**So when you give to the poor**, do*
not sound a trumpet before you, as the hypocrites do in the
synagogues and in the streets, so that they may be honored
*by men. Truly I say to you, **they have their reward in full.***

But when you give to the poor, "__do not let your left hand__ __know what your right hand is doing, so that your giving__ __will be in secret; and your Father who sees what is done__ __in secret will reward you__.

(Mat 6:1-4)

Did you notice that Jesus did not mention anything about giving to a **__pastor or a church__**, but did mention about giving to the poor twice in this scripture? Did you also notice that Jesus gave instruction to do your giving in **__secret__** so others would not be aware of what you gave and to whom?

Have you ever noticed how some pastors will buddy up to the **__big__** **__tither__**? Like someone who makes a **__lot of money__** or who is worth a **__lot of__** **__money__**? Have you ever noticed how excited some pastors get when a financially **__well to do person__** visits or joins their church? Then compare that to the way those pastors treat some **__poor person__** who has little or nothing to give. Why do you think there is a **__difference__**? Isn't it really just about the **__money__**? I challenge you think about it and look for yourself. **__Is__** **__this the way of Jesus__**?

So how would you judge the modern teaching on giving and tithing? Is it a biblical **__truth or a myth__**?

The Myth of the Paid Pastor

The question is not how much should a preacher be paid, but if he should be paid at all for doing what God has gifted and called him to do? There are a variety of gifts and ministries given to the church by the Holy Spirit for the common good of the Body. Why should only the pastor's gift and a few staff members be paid for their gifts, when all the other members serve on a **_voluntary basis_**? Who decided that? Why are the pastors at the top of the list of those getting salaries? Didn't the apostles and Jesus teach that we should not show partiality, and that even the less seemly members be given more abundant honor so that all members would be recognized as necessary? Didn't Jesus say that the greatest among you would be the **_servant of all_**, not the highest paid of all? Why is there **_no record_** in the Bible of any **_righteous man_** ever being paid for their service to God and His people?

Not only did they not receive pay, but they **_actually refused_** to take anything from the people to whom they brought the Word of God. Righteous men **_clearly understand_** that when they are paid by the very people to whom they are to bring the Word of God, that the money will eventually affect the message, and the messenger will end up **_pleasing the people_** rather than God. The Lord understands human nature, so He **_never intended_** for men to receive money for preaching His Word. But Isn't that what we have today? Paid preachers giving smooth, **_ear-tickling messages_** that keep everyone comfortable in their sins? Where is the preacher who is free from the approval of man and the love of sordid gain (money others have worked for)? Where is the preacher who will confront the sin in the church and call the members to repentance? Read on and see if the idea that a preacher should be paid is a ***biblical truth or myth***!

In the nineties, I once had a discussion with one of my vendors at my business. He told me that his pastor was ***paid six figures*** at his church, plus various other financial benefits including an expense account, clothing expenses, insurance, retirement, and an occasional love offering for vacation, etc. I said that he must really preach a lot for that kind of money and benefits. He said, "Oh yes, he preaches for about ***thirty minutes*** on Sunday morning, about ***thirty minutes*** on Sunday night and about ***thirty minutes*** on Wednesday night."

I said, "Wow, so he only preaches one and a half hours per week for ***all that money*** plus all the other benefits?"

He said, "Well, he does more than that."

I said, "Like what?"

He said, "Well, he prays and studies his Bible."

I said, "So you pay him for that? Shouldn't everyone do that?"

He said, "Well, he does more than that."

I said, "Like what?"

He said, "Like, visits the sick in the hospital."

So, I responded to him this way: "Now let me get this straight. You (your church) pay your pastor $100,000 plus benefits per year, to only preach an hour and a half per week, study his Bible ***for you***, do your praying ***for you*** and visit ***your sick friends*** in the hospital instead of you going to see them yourself?"

I told him that I preached a lot more than that ***for free***, ***studied my own Bible*** and did ***my own praying*** and when one of my friends got sick, ***I visited them myself***. And doing all that while I worked fifty to sixty hours per week in my business. I told him he ***could not hire*** someone to take away ***his responsibility*** to know God, to know his Word, to pray to

God and visit the sick for himself. He became very **_offended_**. Have you ever thought about this type of thing? Does it make any sense to you? Have you studied the Bible to see what it says for yourself?

There is **_no case_** in the Bible of any **_righteous_** man of God ever making a **_vocation_** (job for pay) out of preaching the Word of God and this **_will be proven_** as you read this chapter.

Notice what Jesus told his disciples concerning getting paid when they preached:

> *And as you go, preach, saying, 'The kingdom of heaven is at hand.' "Heal the sick, raise the dead, cleanse the lepers, cast out demons; freely you received, freely give. Do not acquire gold, or silver, or copper for your money belts, or a bag for your journey, or even two tunics, or sandals, or a staff; for the worker is worthy of his support.*
> (Matt. 10:7–10)

Notice that the first thing Jesus told them was "**_freely you received, freely give._**" That clearly means the gospel did not cost them anything and they **_could not charge_** anything for preaching what was given to them for free! Who changed that?

The second thing Jesus told them was "**_do not acquire_** (get or take) gold, silver or copper for your money belts." In other words, these men with mission assignments were not to take any money along with them.

Just as Jesus told them (in Luke chapter ten) that they would have their **_necessities_** provided for. Having necessities provided for while on a mission trip away from home is a much different than charging for the gospel or preaching as a pastor **_for money_** at home.

The third thing Jesus said was that the worker was worthy of his **_support_**. This seems strange after saying "freely you received, freely give," until we study a little further. The Greek word used here for support is **_trophe_**, which means **_physical nourishment_** for the body, as in getting to **_eat food_**. These apostles were allowed to **_eat food_** when traveling away from their homes to preach. So, food, shelter, etc., was their support, **_not money_**! Apparently, the reason they were allowed to eat food away from home was because they were away from their normal ability to provide food for themselves as they usually did. Why don't men who study the Bible and who went to Bible school or seminary **_tell us this_**?

Jesus also told his disciples this when he sent them out to preach—

> *"Go your ways; behold, I send you out as lambs in the midst of wolves. "**_Carry no purse_**, no bag, no shoes; and greet no one on the way. "And whatever house you enter, first say, 'Peace be to this house.' "And if a man of peace is there, your peace will rest upon him; but if not, it will return to you. "And stay in that house, **_eating and drinking_** what they give you; for the laborer is **_worthy of his wages_**. Do not keep moving from house to house. "And whatever city you enter, and they receive you, **_eat what is set before you_**."*
> (Luke 10:3–8)

Again, the wages for preaching, when you travel away from home, are only **_food and shelter_** and any reasonable personal necessities you might have while on the trip. The wages spoken of in Luke 10 are not what we would normally associate with as the wages of today, and they certainly are **_NOT ABOUT MONEY_**!

Here again, Jesus clearly tells them to **_carry no purse_**. You see they did not need a purse if they were not going to collect any money. Nor did they need a purse to pay for food and lodging if they were going to stay in somebody's house with all necessities provided for them. Also, Jesus again made it clear that their wages were **_food, drink, and lodging_**, etc.

No money was associated with these "wages" or "support," only **_basic necessities_**. In fact, they were forbidden to receive money for doing what God called them to do!

So, do you see how **_traditions_** handed down to us from the past have **_invalidated_** the Word of God and made it to no effect? What preacher have you ever heard preach these scriptures, explaining that the support and wages for the preacher were not money? But was only food for the **_traveling preacher_**, who was allowed to stay and eat at someone's home but was not allowed to collect any money? So, it is obvious that the preacher/pastor is not allowed to **_take money_** for doing the work of God.

In 2 Kings 5, Elisha the prophet of God **_refused to receive money_** from Naaman after he was healed of leprosy. But Elisha's servant Gehazi took two talents of silver and two changes of clothes from Naaman without Elisha's knowledge. When Elisha discovered what Gehazi had done he said:

> Then he said to him, "Did not my heart go with you, when the man turned from his chariot to meet you? Is it a time to **_receive money and to receive clothes and olive groves and vineyards and sheep and oxen and male and female servants_** (for doing the work of God)? "Therefore, the leprosy of Naaman shall cleave to you and to your descendants forever." So, he went out from his presence a leper as white as snow. (2 Kings 5:26–27)

So Gehazi was cursed **_for accepting money_** and other benefits for the work of God done through Elisha. Wasn't the gift of God freely received and shouldn't it be **_freely given_**? Elisha made it clear that it was not acceptable to receive material gifts or financial compensation of any kind for doing what God had called him to do. And Gehazi's descendants are the ones who do what he did and receive pay for serving in the ministry. His descendants are with us today! And they are unclean just like one with leprosery is.

So how many pastors/preachers/televangelists/priests are under a **_curse_** today for **_taking money_** for doing what they say God called them to do? Yet they **_don't even know_** that they are cursed!

Another point here is that the church is not to be governed by a **_single pastor_**. The church is supposed to be governed by a **_body of elders_**. These are seasoned **_older men_** who are often called overseers. Notice that Paul always appointed elders (**_plural_**), not a pastor (singular), to manage the new church. The idea of one man leading the church probably came from the "pope" mentality of the Catholic Church and stayed with the Protestant movement making the pastor the head of the church. These elders should function in their different gifts as apostles, pastors, evangelists, prophets and teachers. Jesus **_never intended_** that one man could exercise all the gifts necessary for the building up of the body until it becomes mature, to the measure and stature that belongs to Christ. This probably won't happen unless all the provided gifts are working. And none of these gifted men should be paid for this.

Preaching is not a **_vocation_**, but a gift and a calling to service. Congregations should not be very large and should have multiple leaders acting as **_elders/overseers_** to help equip the saints. If the overseers work for a living and teach and equip the saints in their time off from work, the church will be **_much better off_**. Today, we have a church system with mostly one pastor managing programs, entertainment, staff, finances, building maintenance, construction, budgets, marketing, weddings, funerals, and very often, hundreds if not thousands, of members. The church is now run like a business and the pastor acts as the CEO. This is not really for the discipling and equipping of the saints Jesus intended. One elder can only disciple a **_few families_**. Several elders can disciple several families. What if some elders left the large church situation and began home churches with one or two elders in each home, who worked for a living, and discipled small numbers of members in their homes? It would all be free, no salaries, no construction, no budgets, no marketing, no paid staff, and ***no one left out of being discipled***!

Even if a larger group had to rent some meeting space, this would be ***fairly inexpensive***, compared to paying pastors and staff members and building large, expensive buildings. During the last thirty-eight years, I have discipled ***many couples*** and individuals ***without pay***. All the while, I owned and operated an auto repair business full-time. I also raised a family and spent a lot of time ***studying the Word of God***. You see, anyone can find time for what they love to do. Some men love hunting, ***football***, camping or fishing and spend a ***lot of time and money*** on these things, while working a full-time job. It just depends on where your heart is.

What if a man loved God and wanted to make a difference for the Kingdom of God? Couldn't he find time after working for a living, to serve the Lord and do it ***without pay or compromising the truth***? After all, there are 168 hours in a week. If forty hours were spent working for a living, and fifty-six hours spent sleeping, that still leaves seventy-two hours to do something with. This is the time we choose what we do. Of course, some time is for family, some for marriage, and some for personal use, but still we could salvage maybe one fourth of the seventy-two hours for God and maybe use eighteen hours a week for study, teaching, discipling and building up the Kingdom of God. I dare say that ***very few paid pastors*** invest that much time each week in ***actually serving God*** by personally working in the ***lives of others***. Their time and attention is ***devoured*** by church "business," religious programs, building programs, marketing programs, budgets, planning ceremonies, directing staff, going to speaking engagements (***of no real importance to God***), boosting their ministry, counseling unrepentant members and doing little to ***no real work at all***. All this worthless "work" is done while living the life of the "***clergy***" and looking for the respectful greetings in the "marketplaces" and the "chief seats" in the "temples." So, a godly man could easily __work for a living__, and do lots of __worthwhile work__ for the Kingdom of God, __without being paid__ as a pastor.

> *And He gave some as apostles, and some as prophets, and some as evangelists, and some as pastors and teachers, __for the equipping of the saints for the work of service,__ to the building up of the body of Christ; until we all attain to the __unity of the faith__, and of the knowledge of the Son of God, to a __mature man__, to the measure of the stature which belongs to the fullness of Christ. As a result, __we are no longer to be children__, tossed here and there by waves and carried about by __every wind of doctrine__, by the trickery of men, by craftiness in deceitful scheming; but speaking the truth in love, we are to grow up in all aspects into Him who is the head, even Christ, from whom the whole body, being fitted and held together __by what every joint supplies__, according to the proper working of __each individual part__, causes the growth of the body for the building up of itself in love.* (Eph. 4:11–16)

In Numbers chapter 16, Moses, a servant of God, had to deal with the rebellion of Korah. Korah and several men rose up against Moses and his leadership and rebelled against him. When Moses cried out to God he said—

> *Then Moses became very angry and said to the Lord, "Do not regard their offering! __I have not taken__ a single donkey __from them__, nor have I done harm to any of them."* (Num. 16:15)

As minister and leader of God's people, Moses could say with confidence that he had **_taken nothing_** from any of the people, not even a donkey. Therefore, Moses had not been tempted to please the people but was free to say only what God was saying. Some did not like it and rebelled against him. It is very hard—no, virtually impossible for men to **_take money_** and gifts from their members and still please God, because they will end up **_pleasing the people_** instead. When men are paid to preach, it is extremely difficult if not impossible for them to be objective and preach only what God says **_especially if the people don't like it_**! Moses stayed clear of any temptation to compromise what God was saying to the people, by never taking anything from them. How rare it is today to find this kind of integrity in a minister. This kind of integrity refuses to take anything from the people and serves the people and God because it is **_in his heart to do so_**, not because he makes a living doing it. This should be a lesson for us today.

The faithful prophet of God, Samuel, had this to say about being paid—

> *"And now, here is the king walking before you, but I am old and gray, and behold my sons are with you. And I have walked before you **from my youth even to this day.** "Here I am; bear witness against me before the Lord and His anointed. **Whose ox have I taken, or whose donkey have I taken, or whom have I defrauded**? Whom have I oppressed, or from **whose hand have I taken a bribe to blind my eyes with it**? I will restore it to you." And they said, "**You have not defrauded us, or oppressed us, or taken anything from any man's hand**." And he said to them, "The Lord is witness against you, and His anointed is witness this day **that you have found nothing in my hand."** And they said, "He is witness." (1 Sam. 12:2–5)*

So, Samuel spent his whole life as a preacher of the Word of God in Israel and he _**never took anything from any man**_. Not even a single gift, offering or benefit of any kind. Samuel indicated that if he had taken anything, then he would have received a _**bribe,**_ and it would have _**blinded his eyes**_. I wonder how many men down through the ages have had their _**eyes blinded by taking money and gifts for preaching**_. There is no doubt that this compromise is the standard for the American "Christian" church today.

Here is how it works. The preacher/pastor receives money and gifts from the ones he is supposed to be _**instructing in right living**_. He is supposed to be _**correcting those who do wrong**_, and he is supposed to be _**rebuking those who continue to do wrong**_ and he is supposed to be _**removing those from the church who won't repent**_. But having taken the money and gifts from the very people he is supposed to be _**holding to an account for their sins**_, he will turn a _**blind eye**_ to their sins and will refrain from confronting them for their sins. So, in order to keep his _**customers**_ (church members) happy and keep them coming back and the money flowing, he will have to go easy on them and eliminate correcting and rebuking sinful behavior. Therefore, his messages will be mostly ear tickling in nature and he will say things like "_**we are all just sinners saved by grace**_" or "_**we are just going to love everybody here**_" or "_**it is not the personality of this church to correct people**_,". He will do this in order to _**excuse the sins of the people**_. He will then teach the _**popular false doctrines**_ of the day which "allow" people to feel _**comfortable in their sins**_, causing them to believe that they are going to heaven while they live in a _**carnal lifestyle**_. And since his eyes are _**blinded by the bribe**_ of receiving money and gifts from the very "members" he is supposed to be guiding away from living in sin, he now accepts the sins of the people as a _**normal part of being a Christian**_. And since he himself is _**blind**_ to the dangers of sin, he will lead the people to the ***pit of hell***, along with himself.

> *And He also spoke a parable to them: "A **blind man** cannot*
> *guide a blind man, can he? Will they not **both fall** into a*
> *pit?" (Luke 6:39)*

I wonder how many ***millions*** of people are in hell right now because they listened to a ***paid preacher*** tell them that they were alright with God. This is certainly going on today more than ever before, because the church in America is full of ***people practicing sin***. It is clear in the Bible that if you willfully practice sin that you are on the ***way to destruction***. And what funeral did you ever go to that the ***paid preacher*** didn't preach the deceased person right on into heaven, even though everybody knew how he or she really lived here on the earth? You see, this very practice itself gives people a false hope and a ***false sense of security***.

Speaking of false teachers, Jude had this to say—

> *Woe to them! For they have gone the way of Cain, and **for***
> ***pay they have rushed headlong into the error of***
> ***Balaam** and perished in the rebellion of Korah. (Jud. 1:11)*

If you study Balaam, he was a man who knew God, but he was willing to compromise and preach against what God had said for the ***money he was paid***. The ***money blinded his eyes,*** and he was willing to make compromises because of it. In other words, he preached what the people who paid him wanted him to say, ***for the money***. Again, this is a warning for the present time!

Paul the apostle said this—

For it is written in the Law of Moses, "You shall not muzzle the ox while he is threshing." God is not concerned about oxen, is He? Or is He speaking altogether for our sake? Yes, for our sake (preachers) it was written, because the plowman ought to plow in hope, and the thresher to thresh in hope of sharing the crops. If we sowed spiritual things in you, is it too much if we should reap material things from you? If others share the right over you, do we not more? Nevertheless, we __did not use__ this right, but we endure all things, that we may cause no hindrance to the gospel of Christ. Do you not know that those (Levitical priest) who perform sacred services eat the __food of the temple__, and those who attend regularly to the altar have their share with the altar (tithe)? So also, the Lord directed those who proclaim the gospel to get their __living from the gospel__. (1 Cor. 9:9–14)

So, Paul made it clear that according to the law, that he as a minister, had a right to receive material things when he had sown spiritual things. Again, he wasn't talking about a salary, love offerings, money, or other valuable assets, but simply about __*food*__. Just like those who were able to __*eat the food*__ at the temple. This was the living he was referring to: food, drink and shelter. But notice that Paul did not __*USE*__ his right to __*EAT food*__ without paying for it. He said that he did not want to cause any hindrance to the gospel of Christ. Could it be the __*concern*__ Paul had for the bribe principle, blinding one's eyes from being straightforward to the ones from whom you are receiving food or any other benefits? Where is the preacher __*like this today*__? Most preachers I know, not only want to be paid, but expect others to __*pay for their meals*__ when they go out to dinner.

What makes a preacher think he should be treated in a **_special_** way? The word "clergy" is not in the Bible. Why should a preacher be paid or have his own special parking place? Isn't this kind of treatment reserved for **_kings_** and princes of the world? Didn't Jesus say that the greatest among you would be the **_servant of all_**?

Again, notice what else Paul had to say about this:

> *Now we command you, brethren, in the name of our Lord Jesus Christ, that you keep aloof from every brother who leads an **unruly life** and not according to the tradition which you received from us. For you yourselves know how you ought to **follow our example**, because we did not act in an undisciplined manner among you, **nor did we eat anyone's bread without paying for it**, but with labor and hardship **we kept working night and day** so that we might not be a burden to any of you; not because we do not have the right to this, but in order to offer ourselves as a model for you, **that you might follow our example.** For even when we were with you, we used to give you this order: **if anyone** (including preachers) **will not work, neither let him eat**. (2 Thess. 3:6–10)*

Paul was a preacher and a tent maker. Paul **_did not_** consider preaching to be a vocation. **_No one_** in the Bible had a vocation of preaching. Paul's vocation was **_making tents_**. He had freely received the gospel from the Lord, and **_for free_**, Paul preached it. Even though Paul had a right **_to eat food_** as a minister of the gospel, he **_did not exercise that right_**. That right **_was never about taking money_** or being paid as a preacher, but only about whether or not he would eat someone else's food. In fact, Paul did not eat without paying for his food and he admonished all ministers to **_follow his example in this_**. This is New

Testament instruction! Again, see how far we have drifted from the will of God and from what the Scriptures teach!

Jesus said this concerning pastors/shepherds—

> *"Truly, truly, I say to you, he who does not enter by the door into the fold of the sheep but climbs up some other way (by being paid), he is a **thief and a robber**. "But he who enters by the door is a shepherd (true pastor) of the sheep. "All (pastors/shepherds) who came before Me are **thieves and robbers**, but the sheep did not hear them. "I am the door; if anyone enters through Me, he shall be saved, and shall go in and out, and find pasture. "**The thief comes only to steal, and kill, and destroy**; I came that they might have life and might have it abundantly. "I am the good **shepherd**; the good **shepherd** lays down His life for the sheep. "**He who is a hireling**, (paid pastor) and not a **shepherd** (pastor), who is not the owner of the sheep, beholds the wolf (in sheep's clothing) coming, and leaves the sheep (in the wolf's teaching), and flees (from what is right), and the wolf snatches them, and scatters them. "He flees because he is a **hireling** (paid pastor) and is **not concerned** about the sheep." (John 10:1–2, 8–12)*

Here, Jesus said, that the shepherd (pastor) who is financially compensated for his duties as a pastor is a **hireling**, and that a hireling (**a paid pastor**) is **not the shepherd of God's sheep**. This hireling is far more concerned with **his income** and reputation than he is about the souls of the sheep. Hirelings allow the false teachings of **wolves in sheep's clothing** to snatch the sheep. Can you accept what Jesus said? He didn't give any exceptions to this, so can you?

The thief who came to steal, kill, and destroy in this passage, is **_not Satan_,** as most pastors have taught us, but **_the thief_** is **_the paid pastor_** (hireling) himself! The topic here is about **_shepherds_** (pastors), not Satan as most pastors teach. A pastor who comes into the fold of the sheep by some other way (by being paid), other than the door (Jesus) by taking money for preaching, is a **_thief and a robber_**. This paid pastor is not like Paul, Elisha, Samuel, Moses, John, Peter, or any other righteous men of God. This pastor loves sordid gain (**_money he did not work for_**). These pastors rob members of their money to pay themselves and in the process, steal the member's **_souls_** because they tickle ears and compromise the Word of God in order to keep their pay. These shepherds leave out the **_judgments and warnings of God_** and preach "**_easy believism_**," or "**_false grace_**", and they give a **_false hope_** of salvation to their members. These paid pastors teach some form of "peace and safety" to people who still live in sin. Every time someone dies, **_the hireling always_** "preaches" them to heaven, tickling the ears of everyone at the funeral.

Also, these hirelings don't teach about the **_narrow way_** and how few enter eternal life. They leave out total repentance from sin, bearing one's own personal cross, and self-denial of sin and worldliness, which all are required for salvation. The hireling leaves the impression that virtually everyone in church, and even many outside the church, go to heaven, even though Jesus plainly taught that only just a **_few will enter life_**. The hireling will pervert grace and turn it into a **_license to sin_**. The reason they do this is because they are hirelings. Hirelings are paid preachers blinded by bribes (financial gain) and the traditions of men. Hirelings are the ones who continually preach about **_tithing_**, even though they should know that tithing never was about money and has nothing to do with the church. They preach tithing because it is the source of their **_income_**. Hirelings **_are not_** the shepherds of God. If you can be hired, you **_can be fired_**! Who could have ever fired Paul, Peter, Jesus, Samuel, Moses,

Elijah, John the Baptist or any other man of God? It is the hireling, the paid shepherd (pastor) who came to ***steal, kill and destroy***! He will steal your money, your family, your time and your soul by leaving out the warnings of God and the sense of urgency, while ***keeping you busy*** with religious activity so you will miss knowing God or His will for your eternal life.

> *Therefore, I exhort the elders among you, as your fellow*
> *elder and witness of the sufferings of Christ, and a partaker*
> *also of the glory that is to be revealed,* ***shepherd*** *the flock*
> *of God among you, exercising oversight* ***not under***
> ***compulsion, but voluntarily, according to the will of***
> ***God;*** *and* ***not for sordid gain****, but with eagerness; nor yet*
> *as lording it over those allotted to your charge, but proving*
> *to be examples to the flock. And when the Chief Shepherd*
> *appears, you will receive the* ***unfading crown*** *of glory. (1*
> Pet. 5:1–4)

Here, Peter plainly says for the shepherd (pastor) to serve ***voluntarily*** according to the will of God (which is without pay) and ***not for sordid gain*** (taking money others have worked for). If he shepherds in this way (without pay) and voluntarily, ***only then*** will he receive his ***unfading crown*** of glory when Jesus comes. So where does that leave the hireling when Jesus comes?

Here is a more complete definition of ***unjust/sordid gain***—To gain or profit from the ***assets or work of others***, to take money you ***did not earn***, to gain from stealing, extortion or ***deception***. It is also called filthy lucre, dirty money, and ***dishonest gain***.

When preachers teach and preach the tithe and that pastors should be paid, they are ***preaching a lie*** and personally gain from the ***deception*** of it. As a result, they ***manipulate*** the hearer into giving at least ten percent by putting him under the pressure that he has to give according to the letter of the law, or he could be cursed. Even if the member is struggling financially, he is **_pressured_** to give the required ten percent tithe anyway. Some churches now have credit card terminals in the pews. The push is always for **_money_**, **_money_** and more **_money_**. This is nothing more than **_extortion_** by the pastors and is very evil. Many widows and poor people have been devastated by this. Television preachers **_promise wealth and healing_** if only you will send them your **_money_**. And when any pastor brings in a special speaker, he again pressures the members to give big so his **_preacher buddy_** will gain a big profit off the **_member's hard-earned income_**.

And have you ever noticed if there is an **_ungodly member_** who is a "big tither", how the pastor will chum up to him and never address his sin? And the pastor always has time and attention for anything the "**_big tither_**" wants. But if some **_poor person_** needs help from the pastor, he or she has to make an appointment and gets **little attention**.

It is like this:

> *For if a man comes into your assembly with a **_gold ring_*** *and **_dressed in fine clothes_**, and there also comes in a* *poor man in dirty clothes, and you **_pay special attention_** to* *the one who is wearing the fine clothes, and say, "You sit* *here in a good place," and you say to the poor man, "You* *stand over there, or sit down by my footstool," have you not* *made distinctions among yourselves, and become judges* *with **_evil motives?_** (Jas. 2:2–4)*

The scriptures plainly tell us that a leader/overseer/shepherd/ pastor/minister is to not be given over to sordid/unjust gain because it blinds their eyes—

*His watchmen are **blind,** all of them know nothing. All of*
*them are **mute dogs** unable to bark (barking is for*
warning), Dreamers lying down, who love to slumber;
*And the dogs are **greedy,** they are not satisfied. And they*
*are **shepherds who have no understanding;** They have*
*all turned to their own way, **Each one to his unjust gain,***
to the last one. (Isa. 56:10–11)

Pastors are supposed to be **watchmen,** protecting and warning the people of **dangers to their souls**, but when they are willing to take **unjust gain** from the people, they become **blind** and then tickle ears to please the people (their source of income) rather than please God by telling the people what **God really wants them to hear**. And since most people **want their ears tickled**, the paid pastors are more than willing to do it **for the money** and the position they desire.

*For the overseer **must be above reproach** as God's*
steward, not self-willed, not quick-tempered, not addicted
*to wine, not pugnacious, **not fond of sordid gain**—*
(Tit. 1:7)

Here are some examples of preachers who have been **excessive** in taking sordid (unjust) gain. Take note of the net worth of some well-known preachers who have spent their lives teaching and preaching tithing, rapture, false grace and eternal security. According to information found on the internet—Charles Stanley, **1.5 million**. He also receives an undisclosed amount by First Baptist of Atlanta and also receives **$299,000** per year from In-Touch Ministries. John Macarthur—**15 million**. He also receives nearly **1 million per year** from his church and Grace to You Ministries. John Hagee, **5 million**—Joel Osteen, **40 million**—Joyce Meyers, **8 million**—Benny Hinn, **42 million**—Billy

Graham, **25 million**—Creflo Dollar, **27 million**—TD Jakes, **18 million**—Pat Robinson, **100 million**—Jerry Falwell Jr., **10 million**—Kenneth Copeland, **787 million**. Plus, there are too many others getting rich to mention.

Besides these preachers, there are thousands and thousands of pastors, preachers, evangelists and Bible teachers with various salaries paid for preaching and teaching what was freely given to them. And the American church is **_no better off today_** with these **_hirelings_**, especially since the church is **_mired down in sin_** and worldliness like **_never before_**. As goes the church, goes the country.

How could it be possible that all these rich preachers took for themselves all that money from the donations given to "their" ministries intended for promoting the gospel, without being guilty of robbery, taking sordid/unjust gain and **_blinding their own eyes_**? Wasn't one of the qualifications for being an overseer of the church, to be free from the **_love of money_** and to not be fond of sordid gain? These **_are not the shepherds of God_**, but hirelings. No humble servant of God could ever take money, much less such huge amounts of money for himself! Not to mention the many hirelings who just take nice **_comfortable salaries_** with benefits each week. Jesus said that the hireling that preaches the gospel for pay is a **_thief and a robber_** who comes only to **_steal, kill, and destroy souls,_** since he is a **_wolf in sheep's clothing_**. Also, you should be concerned at how these men are well spoken of by most everyone. Men who preach the true Words of God are always **_persecuted and slandered,_** just like Jesus, Paul, Moses, Elijah, Jeremiah, Peter, as well as all the messengers of God were in the old days according to the Scriptures. Why would we think it should be any different now?

> *"Woe to you when all men **speak well of you**, for their*
> *fathers used to treat **the false prophets** in the same way."*
> (Luke 6:26)

Look at how popular some men are, like Charles Stanley or Billy Graham or John Macarthur or Benny Hinn or T. D. Jakes or Rick Warren just to name a few. They are **_not hated_** like Jesus or the apostles were for exposing falsehood, not to mention all the prophets who were killed bringing the Word of God to rebellious Israel. Don't we have a rebellious nation now and a modern church that is full of sin and worldliness today? Then why are these men so popular, if they are really saying what **_God is saying_** to a church full of sin and to a rebellious nation like America? These men are not only very popular, but they have **_completely failed_** to address the condition of the church and to call the masses that follow them to **_repentance_**. Yet they have **_taken millions and millions_** from the unsuspecting givers without giving them the slightest lasting **_benefit to their souls,_** and virtually no one seems to notice that they are **_wolves in sheep's clothing_**.

*"The anger of the LORD will not turn back Until He has performed and carried out the purposes of His heart; In the last days you will clearly understand it. "I **did not send** these prophets, but they ran. I **did not speak to them**, but they prophesied. "But if they had stood in My council, then they would have announced My words to My people and **would have turned them back from their evil way** and from the evil of their deeds. "I have heard what the prophets have said **who prophesy falsely in My name**, saying, 'I had a dream, I had a dream!' "How long? Is there anything in the hearts of the prophets who prophesy falsehood, even these prophets of the deception of their own heart, who intend to make My people forget My name by their dreams which they relate to one another, just as their fathers forgot My name because of Baal? "The prophet who has a dream*

*may relate his dream **but let him who has My word speak My word in truth**. What does straw have in common with grain?" declares the LORD. "**Is not My word like fire?**" declares the LORD, "and like a **hammer which shatters a rock**? "Therefore behold, **I am against the prophets**," declares the LORD, "who steal My words from each other. "Behold, I am against the prophets," declares the LORD, "who use their tongues and declare, 'The Lord declares.' "Behold, I am against those who have prophesied false dreams," declares the LORD, "and related them and **led My people astray by their falsehoods** and reckless boasting; yet **I did not send them or command them, nor do they furnish this people the slightest benefit**," declares the LORD.* (Jer. 23:20–22, 25–32)

Jeremiah said that this would happen in the ***last days***. Today's popular prophets, pastors and evangelists are not preaching the Word of God that is like ***fire and a hammer***, but a soft, easy word of false grace, false mercy, false love, and easy "believeism". They also make promises of ***health, wealth, and salvation***, if you give them your money. They leave out the truth about God's ***judgment and wrath*** on disobedient sons. They teach salvation by "sinner's prayer", rather than teach that repentance from sin, bearing fruit and enduring faithful until the end are all necessary for ***eternal life***. Today's popular preachers have changed the very narrow way that leads to life, into a ***broad easy road***, so it now "appears" that virtually anybody can enter in. The gospel has been perverted by today's preachers for ***sordid gain and the approval of men and power***.

Man-made religion has become a ***multi-billion-dollar*** industry, and yet with all this business activity and money, the morals of our nation and the church have only gone down, down, down. ***Let every preacher get a*** ___job___ or start a business, earn his own income and make true disciples of Jesus, rather than false converts. If he can't volunteer to do this ___from his heart___, then he is not fit for service to God!

Notice what Jesus did concerning the merchandising of the things of God:

> *Then they came to Jerusalem. And He entered the temple and began to drive out those who were **buying and selling** in the temple and overturned the tables of the **money changers** and the seats of those who were **selling** doves; and He would not permit anyone to carry merchandise through the temple. And He began to teach and say to them, "Is it not written, 'MY HOUSE SHALL BE CALLED A HOUSE OF PRAYER FOR ALL THE NATIONS'? But you have made it a **ROBBERS' DEN**." (Mar. 11:15–17)*

We now know that the true temple is the heart and body of the true believer, the people of God, not a physical building, and that this house of God, (the true church) is not to have any ___buying and selling___ of the gospel and the Word of God going on within the church. ___No one is to merchandise the things of God,___ nor the gospel of God. No money should be exchanging hands for the things of God. Freely we received, and freely we give. Today we have religious merchandise branded under the name of "Christian" that has become a multi-billion-dollar industry, with countless ministries taking in billions of dollars with countless ministers, staff members, pastors, evangelists, Bible teachers, Bible schools, counselors, Bible professors, etc., receiving pay for having a vocation in the things of God. And they are merchandising countless books, CDs, videos, Bible courses, prayer cloths, holy water, music, anointing oil, promises of healing, promises of wealth, promises of salvation, tickling of ears and whatever else the people want to hear, for the ___profit of money___.

Oh, how Jesus will turn over their "money tables" in judgment. Oh, the judgment on those who have lived the soft, easy lifestyle of the paid minister. These are the ones who are hirelings, who don't shepherd for Jesus, but for money, reputation and the approval of man. **_Woe be to them_** for their judgment will be forever.

Many years ago, I once belonged to a fairly large local church where the pastor had control of the budget. At some point, I got a copy of the budget and discovered that the "senior" pastor paid himself well over six figures per year plus various other financial benefits, bonuses and retirement contributions. What was shocking was that the associate pastor, who was a very hard worker, only got paid about fifteen thousand per year. The associate pastor had a wife and two kids and drove an old Dodge car that was about twenty-five years old. The "**_senior_**" pastor paid himself very well and the associate pastor was living in poverty. This is another case where the **_hireling looks after himself first_** and not the people. Again, the hireling is not a shepherd of God, but is a **_thief and a robber_**.

Notice what the prophet Ezekiel foresaw long ago:

> *Then the word of the LORD came to me saying, "Son of man, prophesy against the shepherds of Israel. Prophesy and say to those shepherds, 'Thus says the Lord GOD, "**_Woe, shepherds of Israel who have been feeding themselves!_** Should not the shepherds feed the flock? "You eat the fat and **_clothe yourselves_** with the wool, you slaughter the fat sheep **_without feeding the flock_**. "Those who are sickly you **_have not strengthened_**, the diseased you **_have not healed_**, the broken you have **_not bound up_**, the scattered you have **_not brought back, nor have you sought for the lost_**; but with force and with severity **_you have dominated them._** "They were scattered for lack of a shepherd, and they*

became food for every beast of the field (demons) and were
scattered. "My flock wandered through all the mountains
and on every high hill; My flock was scattered over all the
surface of the earth, and there was no one to search or seek
for them." "Therefore, you shepherds, hear the word of the
LORD: "As I live," declares the Lord GOD, "surely because My
flock has become a prey, My flock has even become food for
*all the beasts of the field for **lack of a shepherd**, and My*
*shepherds **did not search** for My flock, but rather the*
***shepherds fed themselves and did not feed My flock**;*
therefore, you shepherds, hear the word of the LORD: 'Thus
*says the Lord GOD, "**Behold, I am against the shepherds**,*
and I will demand My sheep from them and make them
cease from feeding sheep. So, the shepherds will not feed
themselves anymore, but I will deliver My flock from their
mouth, so that they will not be food for them."""
(Ezek. 34:1–10)

These shepherds were feeding themselves with ***money***, ***position***, ***ease***, ***honor*** and ***power***, but they ***were not*** looking after the best interest of the sheep. They clothed themselves with wool that was fleeced from the sheep (the member's money and talents). They slaughter the fat sheep (big tithers), who are the ones who can financially support them. They slaughter the fat sheep by telling them that they are going to heaven, even though they live a ***carnal*** lifestyle. They teach them a ***false grace*** that gives a false sense of security. They preach the dead to heaven every time. They ***don't really heal or help*** the rest of the sheep that are ***sick with spiritual problems.*** When the lost leave the church, they don't go and bring them back and try to save them. The broken are no better off with the divorce rate at ***50 to 60 percent*** in the American church. This divorce rate is a ***tragedy***. Families are broken up and the children are scattered to the wind and the pastors **_do nothing about it_**. They rule with force and severity: "if you don't like it you can leave, I am the pastor here" or "don't touch God's anointed." Because of these shepherds who took from the sheep and **_did nothing to heal or help them_**, the sheep were scattered and became food for the beast of the field (Satan and his demons). This is the condition of the church today—an institution **_being devoured by demons_** because of the hireling shepherds who preach for pay and tickle the ears of the people without giving them the **_slightest spiritual benefit_**. *So, she* (the "bride") *has become Babylon the great harlot, a **dwelling place of demons**.*

> *And he cried out with a mighty voice, saying, "Fallen, fallen*
> *is Babylon the great! She has become a dwelling place of*
> ***demons and a prison of every unclean spirit**, and a*
> *prison of every unclean and hateful bird. "For all the*
> *nations (denominations) have drunk of the wine of the*
> *passion of her immorality, and the **kings** (hirelings) of the*
> *earth have committed acts of immorality with her, and the*
> ***merchants of the earth have become rich** by the wealth*
> *of her sensuality." I heard another voice from heaven,*
> *saying, "**Come out of her, my people**, so that you will not*
> *participate in her sins and receive of her plagues; **for her***
> ***sins have piled up as high as heaven**, and God has*
> *remembered her iniquities. "Pay her back even as she has*
> *paid and give back to her double according to her deeds; in*
> *the cup which she has mixed, mix twice as much for her. "To*
> *the degree that **she glorified herself and lived***
> ***sensuously**, to the same degree **give her torment and***
> ***mourning**; for she says in her heart, 'I SIT as A QUEEN AND*
> *I AM NOT A WIDOW and will never see mourning.' "For this*
> *reason, in one day her plagues will come, pestilence and*

*mourning and famine, and **she will be burned up with fire**; for the Lord God who judges her is strong.*
(Rev. 18:2–8)

She, the ***false bride of Christ***, thinks that she will not suffer, because she thinks Jesus is her husband and will save her, but in reality, she is a ***harlot under judgment*** because she is going to bed with the world! She has become a ***massive business*** making the merchants of the earth rich with everything she is selling. She spends billions of dollars on television and radio time. She funds billions of dollars on hirelings and billions of dollars on huge fancy, expensive buildings. There are countless "Christian" bookstores, "Christian musical singers and bands, "Christian" radio and television stations, "Christian" movies and actors, "Christian" comedians, "Christian" counselors, "Christian" ministries, "Christian" missionaries, "Christian" books, "Christian" CDs and DVDs and "Christian" colleges. Not to mention the "holy water", "prayer cloths", "anointing oils" and too many other things to mention that are for sale under the name of "Christian". This doesn't even consider all the big contracts to build new expensive buildings. With all this ***business*** going on, America and the American "Christian" church is still in horrible shape spiritually. The Church is ***morally bankrupt*** and has been taken over by Satan and his demons. The merchants of the earth are ***getting wealthy*** from all this business without the American churches and ministries giving the people who trust in them the ***slightest benefit*** pertaining to the saving of their souls, of overcoming sin and the world.

Also, have you ever noticed the trend for pastors to make their own son the replacement pastor when they retire? Is the church some kind ***dynasty where the son inherits the kingship***? Isn't this like a ***dictator of a third world country*** making his son the heir of his kingdom? It doesn't matter if the son is qualified or called of God, it only matters to the pastor that he can keep the good thing he has going on ***in the family***. So, the ***hireling is like a king***!

The overwhelming majority of today's pastors are hirelings. As a result, the hirelings are elevating themselves ***above*** the rest of the members. They not only expect to be paid well, but also to be ***honored*** and treated special by having ***titles*** used with or substituted for their names.

Jesus made it clear to not treat anyone special—

> *"But they do all their deeds **to be noticed by men**, "They **love the place of honor** at banquets and the **chief seats** in the synagogues, and **respectful greetings** in the market places, and being called Rabbi (or Reverend) by men. "But **do not be called** Rabbi (or pastor); for One is your Teacher, and **you are all brothers**. "**Do not call anyone on earth** your father (as Catholic's do); for One is your Father, He who is in heaven. "**Do not be called leaders** (clergy); for One is your Leader, that is, Christ. "But the **greatest among you shall be your servant**. "Whoever exalts himself shall be humbled; and whoever humbles himself shall be exalted. (Matt. 23:5–12)*

These hirelings love being called "Pastor" or "Doctor" or "Reverend", just like the Pharisees loved to be called "Rabbi." They love the ***respectful greetings*** wherever they go. If these men didn't want to be honored this way, they would not let people use special titles in place of their name or give them ***special honor***. Paul was an apostle, but his name was Paul. A man can be a leader, but his name is not leader. A man can be a pastor, but ***his name is not pastor,*** nor should his name be preceded by "pastor" when someone speaks of him or to him. ***God hates these labels*** that ***separate and elevate*** some men above others.

And it approaches blasphemy for anyone to call a man "**Father**" or "**Reverend**" since **_only God_** is our spiritual Father and only God is to be revered. For your information, the word reverend comes from the word revere, which means to be **_worshiped, revered and feared_**. It also indicates that one is to be honored, adored, and highly respected as **_being most holy_**.

This is the place of honor that is **_only for God_** and not for any man. And we should only fear God and never any man. How dare any servant of God allow anyone to address him as "**_reverend_**". This practice of being titled and honored by men, tells us that they **_are not really of God_** when they allow this to be done for them. According to Jesus, we are **_all brothers_**. There are no men to be specially treated or elevated. Only Jesus is special and worthy of this kind of honor. The greatest man you will ever find is the humble man who **_is a servant_**. We are all called to be servants.

There is no such thing as the "**_clergy_**". This is another title of elevation developed by men to Lord it over the rest of the flock that they have labeled as the "**_laity_**". Neither the word clergy nor laity are found in the Bible, nor are the applications of their meanings. The so-called "clergy" get to park in **_special places_** at the building and the sign is placed there for them. They love the **_best seats_** in the meetings and the **_respectful greetings_** wherever they go. They sometime wear **_special robes_**, **_unique clothing_** or have **_special collars_** to get the attention and respect they desire. They love the **_honor of men_** and the **_unjust gain_** they receive from the members who work for a living. They are acting more like **_kings_** and princes than like humble servants of the people and of God.

Here is the king principle—

*He said, "This will be the procedure of the **king** who will*
*reign over you: he **will take** your sons and place them for*

*himself in his chariots and among his horsemen and they will run before his chariots (church programs). "He will appoint for himself commanders of thousands and of fifties, and some to do his plowing and to reap his harvest and to make his weapons of war and equipment for his chariots. "He **will also take** your daughters for perfumers and cooks and bakers. "He **will take the best** of your fields and your vineyards and your olive groves and give them to his servants. "He will take a tenth (tithe) of your seed and of your vineyards and give to his officers (staff) and to his servants. "**He will also take** your male servants and your female servants and your best young men and your donkeys and **use them for his work** (programs). "He **will take a tenth** of your flocks, and you yourselves will become his servants (doing volunteer work). (1 Sam. 8:11–17)*

So, the pastor/king of today will reign over you as your special leader called the "clergy" or "reverend" or "doctor" or "pastor" or "father" or "priest." He will take your sons, daughters and wives and use them in his programs (without pay). He will appoint **his own** elders and deacons over the members to **do his will**. He will use your sons and daughters for **his own personal benefit**. He will take the **best of your time and energy** for the "church" programs and different ministries. He will take a **tenth of your income** and call it the tithe and **pay himself and pay his staff with it**. Rather than him being your servant bringing the Word of God at no cost to you and turning you from your sins to save your soul, you will end up being **his servant**, giving him your time, energy and money. He will **keep you too busy doing things for the church** for you to focus on your own family or your personal relationship with the Lord. He will praise you before others and call you a "faithful" Christian because **you serve him so well and pay all of your tithes**.

And this pastor/king will focus on ***numbers***, ***dollars*** and ***programs***. For example, he will expect the youth minister to meet a quota of certain numbers or he may fire him and hire someone else to get the numbers he expects. So in order for the youth minister to meet the quota, he will have to ***water down the Word of God*** and ***entertain*** the young people with games and food, rather than teach them truth and the principles that would save their souls. So, today's youth meetings are more about pizza, entertainment, fun and games that ***provide pleasure for the kids***, rather than life giving principles. The truth is that if the youth minister narrowed down the number of kids that he could really work with concerning the things that really matter, he would only have a few. This would result in him losing his job, so he won't do that. In the end, the ***numbers matter*** more than souls, so the end result is that it is just ***business as usual***.

The pastor does the same thing. He must ***market*** to his customers, which are the members of his church. He has to keep the ***numbers up*** and of course the ***offerings*** as well. This is his measure of "success", ***numbers and money***. So, he gives his members what they want, not too much of that boring preaching stuff, and nothing that would make them feel guilty for sinning or make them uncomfortable. His goal is to keep his customers ***happy*** and coming back for more. In fact, he must excel in making people feel good about themselves in order to keep them coming back, even though most of them are deeply ***connected to the world***. And of course, he must provide ***great entertainment*** for his customers, excellent music, special singers, special plays, choir songs, a few good jokes, a reasonable amount of tickling of the ears, and he better keep it all short, so everyone can get to ***lunch on time***. So, if the pastor makes his customers ***happy***, they will be glad to ***pay him*** and ***brag on him*** and keep coming back for more.

Notice this scripture from Paul the apostle—

The word **effeminate** is the Greek word "malakos"— a soft man, a man with soft hands, a man with feminine characteristics, a man unacquainted with manly work. This is **NOT** the same word used for homosexual here, even though some homosexuals are effeminate.

This Greek word "malakos", only appears *four* times in the Bible and is translated one time as *effeminate* and three times as *soft* in the New American Standard Bible. Let us look at the other three times this word was used from the mouth of Jesus—

You see here that Jesus is talking about the ***difference*** between a ***true messenger*** of God, like John the Baptist, vs. a ***soft man*** who lives in a "king's palace," the ***effeminate***. There was ***nothing soft*** about John the Baptist. He ***strongly*** preached ***repentance from sin*** and ***sternly warned*** everyone to bear the fruit of repentance or be cut down. The ***soft king***, of the present time, ***does not preach like John the Baptist did***, but delivers a much ***softer message***. This king (the clergy) of our time lives in the biggest, most **comfortable office** at the church building (***king's palace***) doing ***no manly work*** to earn a living. He is typically a ***soft man*** since He doesn't do anything physically or mentally to ***produce a godly income***. He is following the procedure of the king that the prophet Samuel explained in first Samuel, chapter eight. The ***effeminate*** preaches and collects the tithe, so he can live a ***soft and easy lifestyle***. He also uses the members to run his programs for the church which makes him look good. He loves ***sordid gain***—that is, the money others have worked for. This is the ***hireling*** Jesus talked about in John, chapter ten, who is ***not the shepherd of God***. He is the one who came to ***steal, kill, and destroy***. Yet he is very popular with the people.

I want to be fair, so I must include this with my remarks about the paid preacher. I have no doubt that there are ***a few good***, decent, and godly men serving as a pastor in a few places who are presently being paid for that service. These pastors are ***few and far between***. I am sure these men want to have the best interest of the people at heart and want to please God, but they struggle with being totally straightforward with their members, since they are being supported by these same members that they are required **_to be honest with_**. And since they are not greedy men, they often receive less than they would in a secular job and therefore they are making personal sacrifice for the sake of souls. But they **_did not learn_** this practice from the Bible, but from a **_broken church system_** that has handed down traditions from men, not from God, to them. If they went to Bible school or seminary, they were **_programmed_** to become a paid pastor, expecting to be taken care of **_by the people_** and to be **_set above the people as the "clergy"_**. These good men just didn't know any better than to do as **_they were taught_**. Any paid pastor who has the right heart will read this book and quickly re-evaluate his life and method of being **_paid for preaching_**. He will look for other men in his own church who are qualified elders and teachers and share this responsibility of discipling members with them. **_He will get a job_** and **_move away_** from expensive buildings and budgets, and he will **_simplify the work_** of the church down to discipling people and saving souls, rather than constructing buildings and running programs to keep people happy. In fact, he will move much more toward telling church members that they have no hope, unless they repent of sin and become overcomers, bearing fruit and enduring to the end. As he does this, **_he won't need a large building any longer_**, because **_only the few_** who are really being saved will remain. He will not worry about being popular anymore and will recognize that being paid **_only makes it much harder_** to tell the people what they really need to hear. This good pastor will hear the voice of Jesus and follow after Him and run to the truth **_when he hears it_**.

> _**"No servant can serve two masters;** for either he will hate_
> _the one and love the other, or else he will be devoted to one_
> _and despise the other. You cannot serve God and wealth."_
> _Now the Pharisees, who were lovers of money, were_
> _listening to all these things and were **scoffing at Him**. And_

He said to them, "You are those who justify yourselves in the
*sight of men, but God knows your hearts; **for that which is***
highly esteemed among men is detestable in the sight
***of God**. (Luke 16:13–15)*

If any pastor scoffs at what is written in this book, he is like the Pharisees, who were ***lovers of money*** and being honored by men, and scoffed at these Words of Jesus. He cannot serve both God and money. If the money and his position matter so much he is not fit for service in God's Kingdom. The concept of paying a preacher is ***highly esteemed among men but is detestable in the sight of God***.

"Those who hate the LORD would pretend obedience to
Him, and their time of punishment would be forever."
(Ps. 81:15)

Many, many, many so-called pastors, evangelists, prophets, apostles, and teachers pretend to love the Lord and ***pretend to obey*** the Lord, but if you take away their money, will they still serve the Lord? Will they still serve to disciple people and teach the Word of God ***for free,*** and get a job to pay their own way?

*Thus, says the LORD concerning the **prophets who lead my***
***people astray**; When they have something to bite with*
*their teeth, They cry, "**Peace,**" But against him who puts*
nothing in their mouths They declare holy war.
(Mic. 3:5)

It was a common practice in those days to ***bite gold*** to make sure it was genuine.

So here is a common scenario today—a young man feels called to preach, to become a pastor. He really wants to help people and serve God. He is told he has to go to Bible school or seminary, so he does. There he is **_programed_** with the "**_clergy_**" mindset and taught how he is to be **_above the people_** and how he should be **_taken care of by the people_**. He is also taught various **_traditions of men_** and numerous **_false_** doctrines on salvation. When he graduates, he is **_hired_** by a small church and begins his sincere career as a **_paid pastor_**. At first, he is wholehearted to help everyone **_find God_** and to build up the church. In the beginning, he has to do most everything himself: preach, teach classes, oversee the Sunday school, devise programs, and take care of the budget. As the church grows, he takes in more and more **_money_**, so then there is a need for a building program and added staff members. The more **_numbers_**, he gains, the more **_money_** comes in and the easier it gets for him. Now he can delegate more of the work to other paid staff members and volunteers. He can take a bigger and **_bigger salary_** as the church grows, and soon he is tempted more and more to **_compromise_** with members in sin and to make the messages more and more appealing to the congregation in order to keep up the numbers and the now **_needed income for the larger budget_**. He now understands that numbers translate into **_dollars_**. Therefore, he now preaches a more ear tickling message than he did in the beginning. Now he **_doesn't want to offend anyone_** and lose any numbers. As time goes on, the desire for more numbers and the love of the money **_corrupt the pastor_** and then he becomes an **_effeminate_** (soft) and a hireling at heart. The larger **_numbers_** and taking in more **_money_**, is how he measures his "**_success_**". By this point in time there is not any church discipline to speak of and he has now become a man pleaser rather than a God pleaser. Even though he was not this way in the beginning, he was set up by Satan to fall into this trap, and he will end up in hell (unless he repents) with almost all his members. You see, he was **_corrupted_** by the love of the numbers and the **_love of the money_**. He became **_blinded by taking the bribe_**. These numbers, dollars, "success", and honor **_replaced his first love for God_** and the people, and he fell into the trap of the harlot church system that has **_devoured_** countless ministers and members over the centuries. And it is **_worse today than ever before_**. This is sad and **_extremely serious_**.

So, is the paid preacher/pastor idea as is mostly practiced today, a biblical **_truth or a myth_**?

Don Britton

Christianmyths.org@gmail.com
www.christianmyths.org